MOUNTAIN RESCUE

BY **JAMES YAO**

ILLUSTRATED BY
JACQUELINE DECKER

Glenview, Illinois • Boston, Massachusetts • Chandler, Arizona • Upper Saddle River, New Jersey

Illustrators
CVR, 3-19 Jacqueline Decker; **20** Dan Trush

Photographs
Every effort has been made to secure permission and provide appropriate credit for photographic material. The publisher deeply regrets any omission and pledges to correct errors called to its attention in subsequent editions.

Unless otherwise acknowledged, all photographs are the property of Pearson Education, Inc.

20 Jupiterimages/Brand X/Alamy

ISBN 13: 978-0-328-39497-5
ISBN 10:   0-328-39497-1

The day began with yet another argument between Marisa and her grandmother. Ever since she and her brother, Alvaro, had moved from the city to their grandmother's farm last fall, it seemed that Abuela was always worried that Marisa would get lost or hurt or that something bad would happen.

Marisa, who was nearly 11 years old, wished Abuela would start trusting her more. But with Abuela's constant worrying, Marisa foresaw many more arguments with Abuela.

Marisa felt she had to get away for a while. She prepared for a long hike so that she could be alone. But Abuela insisted that Alvaro go along. Even though Al was 16, Marisa knew more about mountain safety than he did—she had spent last summer hiking and climbing at camp while Al spent his summer vacation playing video games with his friends. Marisa angrily stuffed a backpack with supplies they would need in the mountains: water, a rope, a folding knife, and a sandwich for each of them.

"Let's go, Al," she said, stamping off toward the spectacular mountains of Grand Teton National Park.

"Don't leave the trails!" Abuela called.

How many times are you going to tell me that? Marisa thought. But she answered respectfully. "We won't. We'll be back by dinnertime."

The spring day was so beautiful that Marisa's mood soon improved. The sun sparkled off the snow that still covered Grand Teton peak. A lace of white coated the aspen trees and the air smelled like pine. Who could stay angry on a day like this?

As they crossed the grassy floor of the valley, Al called out, "Look at that!" A herd of bison grazed in the distance. Marisa shifted her backpack on her shoulders and allowed herself a smile. The pack was heavy, but she didn't mind. Things will get better, she decided. She always loved hiking with Al anyway.

Marisa and Al hiked for a few hours, stopping to rest and eat their sandwiches. The argument with Abuela was becoming a distant memory.

As they followed a stream up the side of a ridge in mid-afternoon, Marisa thought she heard a strange sound.

"Stop!" she whispered to Al. Softly, just above the burbling stream, Marisa could hear crying. It was the sound of something small, weak, and—maybe even lost.

"Do you hear it?" she asked. Al shook his head. "Well, I do," she declared. Marisa had to find the source of that sad, scared sound.

She pulled a coil of rope out of her pack and tied one end to a tree. "We'll hold onto this so we don't get lost," she told Al. She led him off the trail toward the edge of the ridge. The crying sound grew louder with each step.

Marisa followed the sound downhill. She did not have to go far. There was a cliff ahead. At the edge of the rocks, Marisa stopped. She felt as if she was about to step off into a void. She lay down on her stomach and peered over the edge.

About fifteen feet below a little lamb lay crying. It was trapped in a small shaft in the rock. It looked up at her and bleated again. Marisa's heart melted to see the poor, trapped little animal. It could not have been very old.

9

"How did it get there?" Al wondered aloud.

"It must have strayed from the flock," Marisa guessed. Abuela's neighbor raised sheep for wool. This must be one of his lambs. "Maybe it slipped on these rocks and fell."

But now what? Marisa wondered. "We'll save you, little lamb," she called down.

"I'll do it," Al said. "I'll rappel down the cliff to get the lamb."

"You?" Marisa asked. "I'm the one who took the climbing course at camp. I should go down the cliff."

"I'm afraid the lamb will be too heavy for you," Al answered. "You can help me get down to it."

Marisa ran back for the rope.

Marisa looped the rope around a tree. Then she tied the other end around Al's waist. She quickly explained to Al how to safely lower himself. She would brace the rope, releasing it slowly to lower him onto the ledge.

Al took a deep breath and began his descent down the cliff. Marisa pressed her hiking boots against a rock and let the rope unwind slowly from around the tree.

In order to return to the top of the cliff, Al had to climb up the rope while holding the lamb. He was breathing hard as he handed Marisa the lamb. It weighed much more than she expected. Marisa gently placed the lamb on the ground beside her.

Then it happened. Al's foot slipped. Marisa grabbed the rope to stop his fall. But it was too late. Al slid back down, twisting his arm in the process.

"Can you climb back up?" Marisa gasped.

"Only with one arm," Al answered, his face twisted with pain.

They struggled as Marisa did her best to pull the rope and grab onto him so he could swing his legs up and climb onto the cliff. Finally, Al was safe. He held his injured arm against his side. Marisa pulled a sweatshirt out of the pack and used it as a sling for Al's injured arm.

Marisa looked at the lamb. "We can't just leave it here," she said. "Another animal will surely find it and eat it." She stroked the lamb's head to calm it while she thought.

Finally, she decided she had no other choice. "I'll have to carry it back," she said. She tried not to think about how many miles it was to Abuela's farm.

Marisa lifted the lamb onto her shoulders. She and Al trekked back down the trail. They moved very slowly. With each step, the lamb felt heavier and Marisa's legs felt weaker and weaker. Her back and shoulders began to ache.

She glanced at the sun above the snowy mountains. It would soon fall behind their peaks. She told Al they had better hurry.

After they had walked several miles, Marisa began to worry about the oncoming darkness. "Abuela will be worried," she breathed, panting as they trudged down the trail. Al said nothing. He was breathing hard as he fought the pain in his shoulder. He kept his head down.

Marisa counted her steps so that she wouldn't think about the ache in her arms and legs. She refused to give up. "Just one foot after the other," she said. Al nodded.

Marisa felt dizzy and began to stagger, her strength nearly gone. As the sun slid behind the mountain peaks, the air seemed to turn purple around her.

A beam of light shot across the valley. But Marisa and Al had their heads down as they strained to keep moving. They did not see Abuela coming towards them, her flashlight darting through the dusk.

Finally, Marisa ran out of strength. She started to stumble when she saw the light of a flashlight ahead moving toward them. She closed her eyes and stopped walking. Al caught up to her as Abuela rushed toward them and took them both in her arms.

Abuela slid the lamb from Marisa's shoulders and set it gently on the ground. Then Abuela helped Marisa to the ground so she could rest.

"Abuela, I'm sorry. I know you must have been worried. This lamb was trapped on a ledge; we had to save it. We couldn't just leave it there, and then Al slipped and hurt his shoulder."

"Oh dear! Are you okay, Al?" Abuela asked.

"I'll be okay, Abuela. Marisa is the one I was really worried about. She's been carrying the lamb for miles," said Al.

"I'm so glad you found us, Abuela," said Marisa.

"I'm just grateful that you're both okay," Abuela said. "I'm very proud of you. You were brave and strong."

"I guess I do need your help sometimes," admitted Marisa.

"It's okay to need help," said Abuela as she handed Marisa and Al each a canteen of water and put blankets around their shoulders. "Sometimes I forget that you are growing up. You are independent like your grandmother. But just know that when you need me, I am here."

"Thanks, Abuela, I know." Marisa struggled to her feet. "Right now I need you to help us bring the lamb back home. And I think Al might need some ice for his shoulder."

"I thought so," said Abuela smiling. "Let's go."

Marisa helped Abuela sling the lamb over her shoulders and the three of them made their way back to the ranch.

Grand Teton National Park

Grand Teton National Park is located in northwest Wyoming, just south of Yellowstone National Park. The two parks are connected by a "wildlife corridor," an area through which wild animals can travel safely.

The Teton Range is just forty miles long, but it is one of the most dramatic and beautiful ranges in the Rocky Mountain chain. This is because the mountains rise steeply from the ground without foothills. The highest point in the park is Grand Teton peak, which is 13,770 feet high.

Today, Grand Teton National Park includes 310,000 acres of wilderness. There are about two hundred miles of hiking trails in the park, and millions of people visit them every year.

Grand Teton
National Park

Grand
Teton

WYOMING